PUFFIN FACTFINDER

NATURAL DISASTERS

Written and edited by
Carol Watson

Consultant
Keith Lye

PUFFIN BOOKS

The consultant, Keith Lye, is a well-known geographer and author of over 90 books for children. He has also acted as consultant on many reference books and atlases.

PUFFIN BOOKS

Published by the Penguin Group
Penguin Books Ltd, 27 Wrights Lane, London W8 5TZ, England
Penguin Books USA Inc., 375 Hudson Street, New York, New York 10014, USA
Penguin Books Australia Ltd, Ringwood, Victoria, Australia
Penguin Books Canada Ltd, 10 Alcorn Avenue, Toronto, Ontario, Canada M4V 3B2
Penguin Books (NZ) Ltd, 182-190 Wairau Road, Auckland 10, New Zealand

Penguin Books Ltd, Registered Offices: Harmondsworth, Middlesex, England

First published 1995
10 9 8 7 6 5 4 3 2 1

Produced for Puffin Books by Zigzag Publishing Ltd, The Barn, Randolph's Farm, Brighton Road, Hurstpierpoint, West Sussex BN6 9EL, England

Senior Editor: Philippa Moyle
Editorial Manager: Hazel Songhurst
Director of Editorial: Jen Green
Designed by Iain Ashman
Illustrated by Peter Bull, Peter Dennis, Iain Ashman and Mainline Design
Cover design: Deborah Chadwick
Cover illustration: Simon Dewey
Production: Zoë Fawcett and Simon Eaton
Series concept: Tony Potter

Colour separations: RCS Graphics, Leeds, England
Printed by Proost, Belgium

Contents

About this book

Every day we read or hear about disasters that happen in the world. Some are accidents that are caused by people, but others are disasters over which we have little control.

This book is about *natural* disasters. A natural disaster is one that happens as a result of changes in the Earth's structure, temperature or weather.

Earthquakes, floods and hurricanes are the most devastating natural disasters and cause many people to die. Others, such as volcanoes, forest fires and avalanches are dangerous, too, but can sometimes be predicted so that people have time to escape.

Finally, there are those disasters that appear to be natural but which may have been caused by human activity polluting or harming the environment.

Earthquakes

An earthquake happens when the surface of the Earth moves suddenly, and without warning. Buildings collapse and people are often buried alive.

We live on the Earth's crust. This is divided into huge plates which glide around very slowly. The most severe earthquakes take place near the edges of these plates.

The size of an earthquake depends on the amount of **pressure** that has been built up along the plates. It can be a small rumble or be so strong it brings down buildings, bridges and roads.

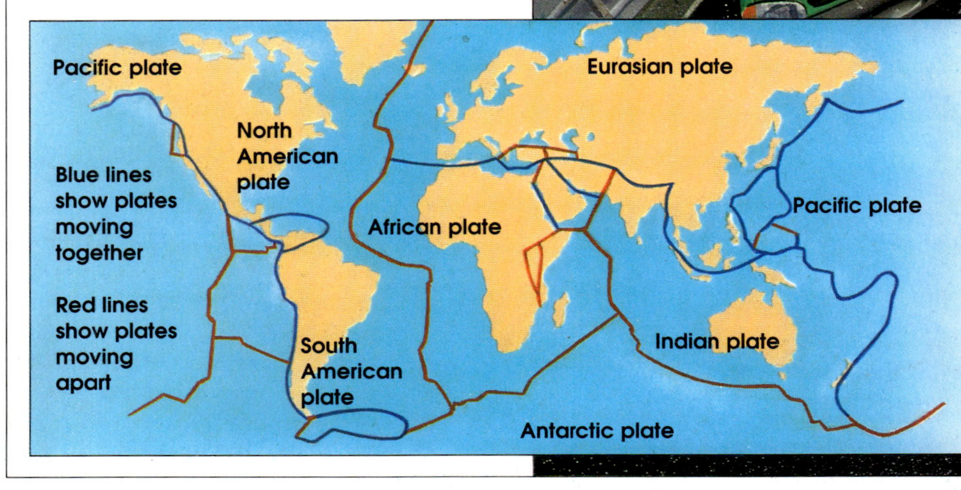

In the middle of the oceans, **plates** move apart and new rock is formed to fill the gaps. This movement causes earthquakes but we do not feel these because they are so far from land.

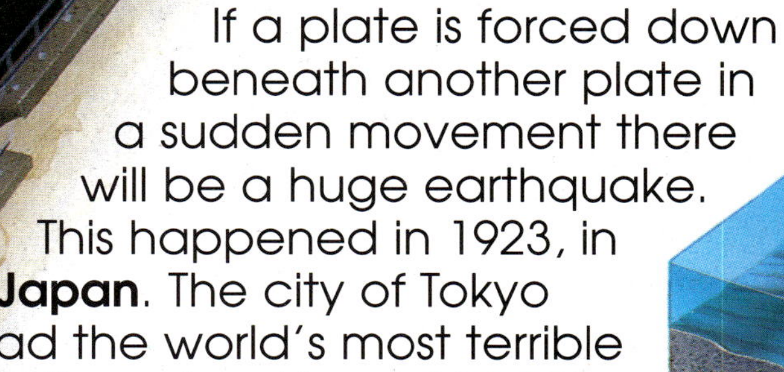

If a plate is forced down beneath another plate in a sudden movement there will be a huge earthquake. This happened in 1923, in **Japan**. The city of Tokyo had the world's most terrible earthquake. About 300,000 buildings were destroyed and approximately 100,000 people were killed.

In January 1995, Japan suffered its worst earthquake since 1923. In the city of Kobe and the surrounding region, over 5,000 people were killed when more than 1,200 buildings were destroyed, motorways collapsed and fires raged throughout the area.

A **fault** is a huge crack that runs across the land where plates move alongside each other.

A fault

The **San Andreas Fault**, in California, US, is where the Pacific Plate and the North American Plate slide past each other. The cities of San Francisco and Los Angeles are in this earthquake zone.

There was a massive earthquake in **San Francisco** in 1906 and another smaller one in 1989. In January 1994, an earthquake in **Los Angeles** killed more than 50 people.

A man called **Dr Charles Richter** devised a scale to measure the force of earthquakes. This is measured on a scale of 1-10. **The Richter Scale** is still used today.

Famous earthquakes *Date*	 *Place*	*Richter value*
1906	San Francisco, US	8.6
1923	Sagami Bay, Japan	8.2
1955	North Assam, India	8.6
1988	Armenia	6.9
1989	San Francisco, US	6.9

Volcanoes

A volcano is a hole in the Earth's crust. When a volcano erupts, hot molten rock from inside the Earth pours out of the hole on to the surface.

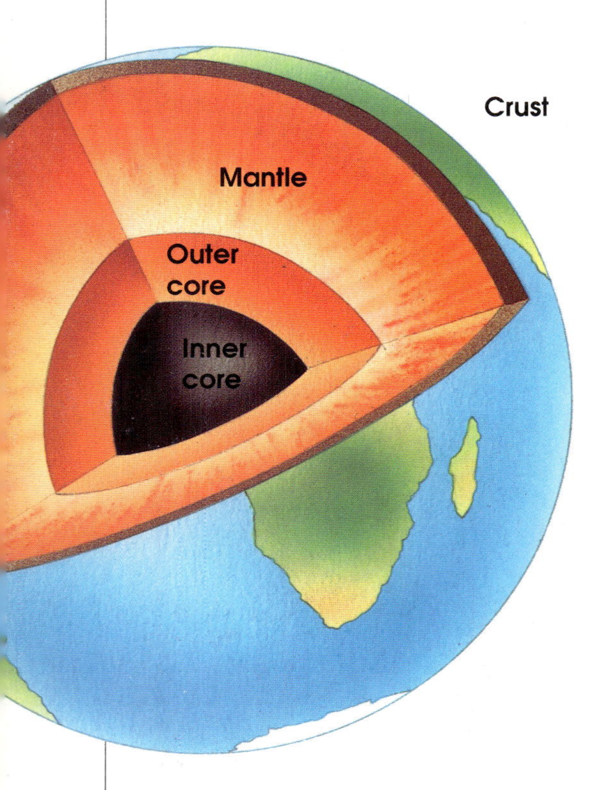

There are two kinds of volcanic eruptions. Some volcanoes explode without warning, and others erupt slowly and quietly, usually allowing time for people to escape.

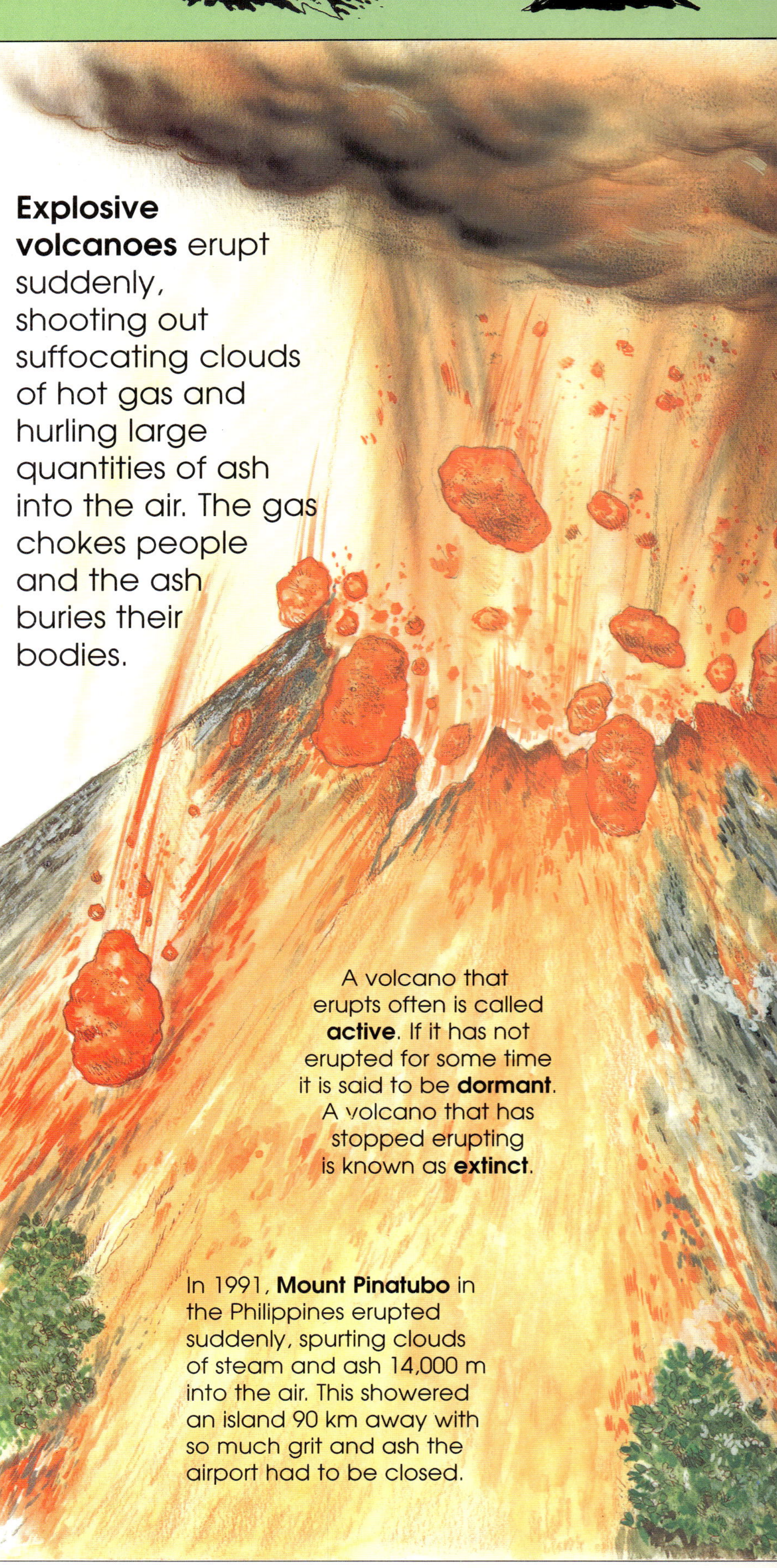

Explosive volcanoes erupt suddenly, shooting out suffocating clouds of hot gas and hurling large quantities of ash into the air. The gas chokes people and the ash buries their bodies.

A volcano that erupts often is called **active**. If it has not erupted for some time it is said to be **dormant**. A volcano that has stopped erupting is known as **extinct**.

In 1991, **Mount Pinatubo** in the Philippines erupted suddenly, spurting clouds of steam and ash 14,000 m into the air. This showered an island 90 km away with so much grit and ash the airport had to be closed.

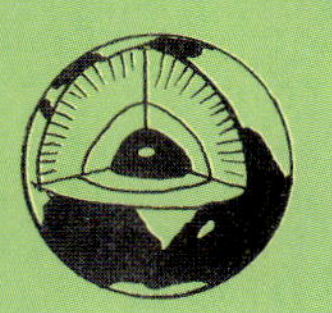

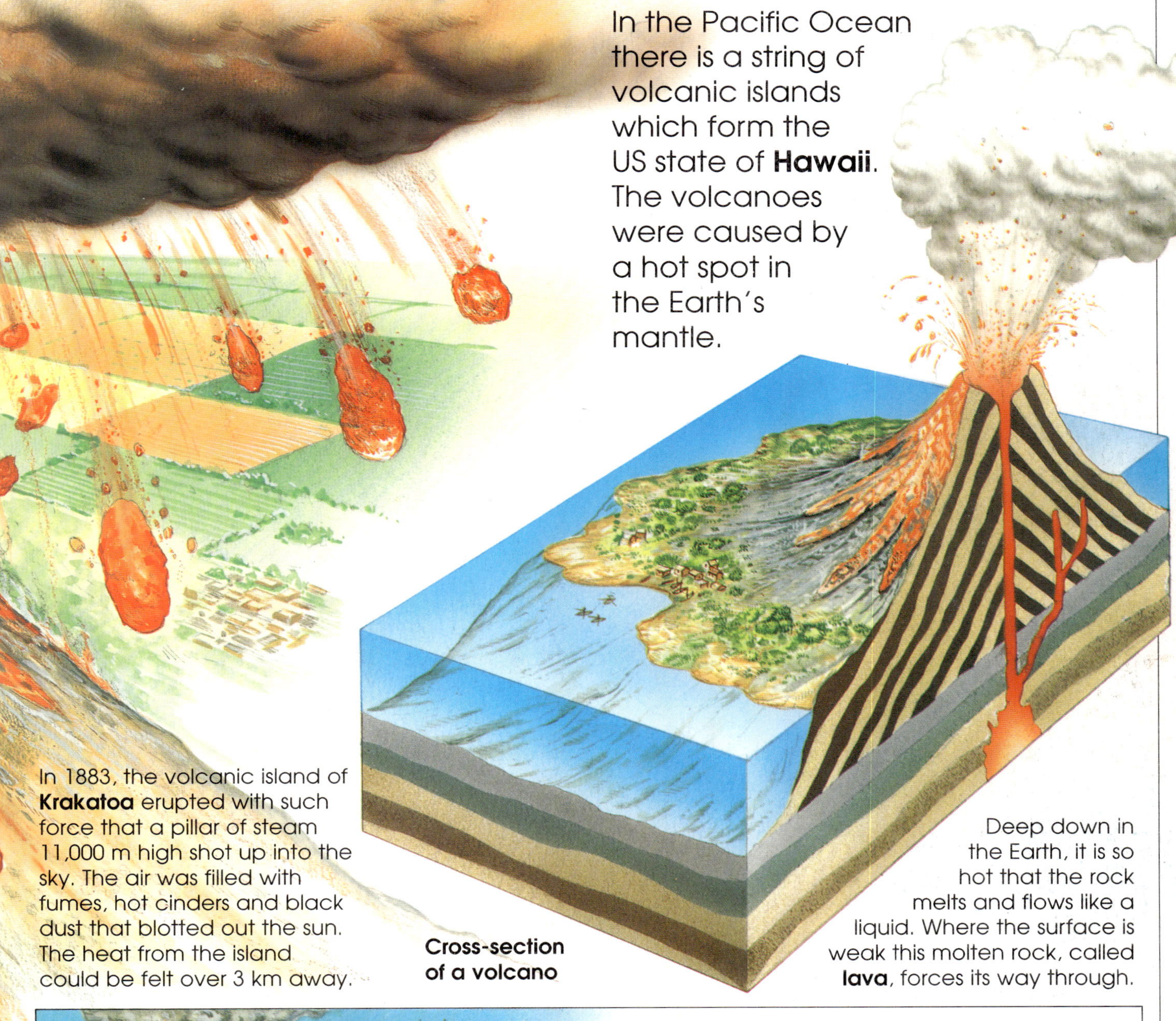

In the Pacific Ocean there is a string of volcanic islands which form the US state of **Hawaii**. The volcanoes were caused by a hot spot in the Earth's mantle.

In 1883, the volcanic island of **Krakatoa** erupted with such force that a pillar of steam 11,000 m high shot up into the sky. The air was filled with fumes, hot cinders and black dust that blotted out the sun. The heat from the island could be felt over 3 km away.

Cross-section of a volcano

Deep down in the Earth, it is so hot that the rock melts and flows like a liquid. Where the surface is weak this molten rock, called **lava**, forces its way through.

Mount Etna, in Sicily, is a volcano that erupts slowly. Long streams of red-hot runny lava flow down the mountainside, burning everything in their path. Mount Etna has been active for 2,500 years. The local people usually have time to escape, but, in 1669, there was an eruption which killed 20,000 people.

Thunder and lightning

Many natural disasters are caused by weather, especially storms. Every day about 45,000 thunderstorms happen somewhere in the world.

A thunderstorm is caused when warm, moist air rises very quickly, forming thunderclouds.

Electrical charges build up inside the clouds. These charges cause flashes inside the clouds, between one cloud and another, or between a cloud and the ground as lightning.

Light travels nearly one million times faster than sound so lightning is seen before thunder is heard.

A flash of **lightning** carries enough electrical energy to light a small city for several weeks. It causes heat five times that of the sun. This makes the air expand and makes a crash of **thunder**.

The safest place to be in a thunderstorm is inside a car, or in a building. Never stand under a tree or hold a metal umbrella.

Thunderstorms sometimes contain **hailstones**. In April 1986, hailstones weighing up to 1 kg killed 92 people in Bangladesh.

In 1959, **Colonel William Rankin** bailed out of his aircraft which had been battered by a thunderstorm in Virginia, USA. As he parachuted down, he was sucked into the heart of the storm. For 40 minutes he was pelted by hailstones, deafened by thunder, and blinded by lightning, but he survived.

Sheet lightning lights up the whole sky.

Forked lightning may reach the ground.

Many buildings have **lightning conductors**. These carry the electricity down into the ground so the building is not damaged. The **Empire State Building** in New York City, USA, is struck by lightning 500 times a year but is protected by a conductor.

In December 1963, 81 people were killed when a **Boeing 707 jet airliner** was struck by lightning in Maryland, USA.

Hurricanes and tornadoes

Hurricanes are the most violent large storms. They form over the warm oceans during the hottest months of the year.

In 1992, **Hurricane Andrew** swept across southern USA. Winds of over 200 km/h made 200,000 people homeless and caused $20,000 million worth of damage in Florida alone. It was the costliest natural disaster in the history of the US.

The high winds of a hurricane become more powerful as they reach land. Some can release the same energy as a volcanic eruption and cause terrible destruction.

A tornado is a smaller storm than a hurricane, but it can have even stronger winds.

In the Atlantic Ocean the storms are called **hurricanes**; in the Indian Ocean they are known as **cyclones**, and in the Western Pacific they have the name **typhoon**.

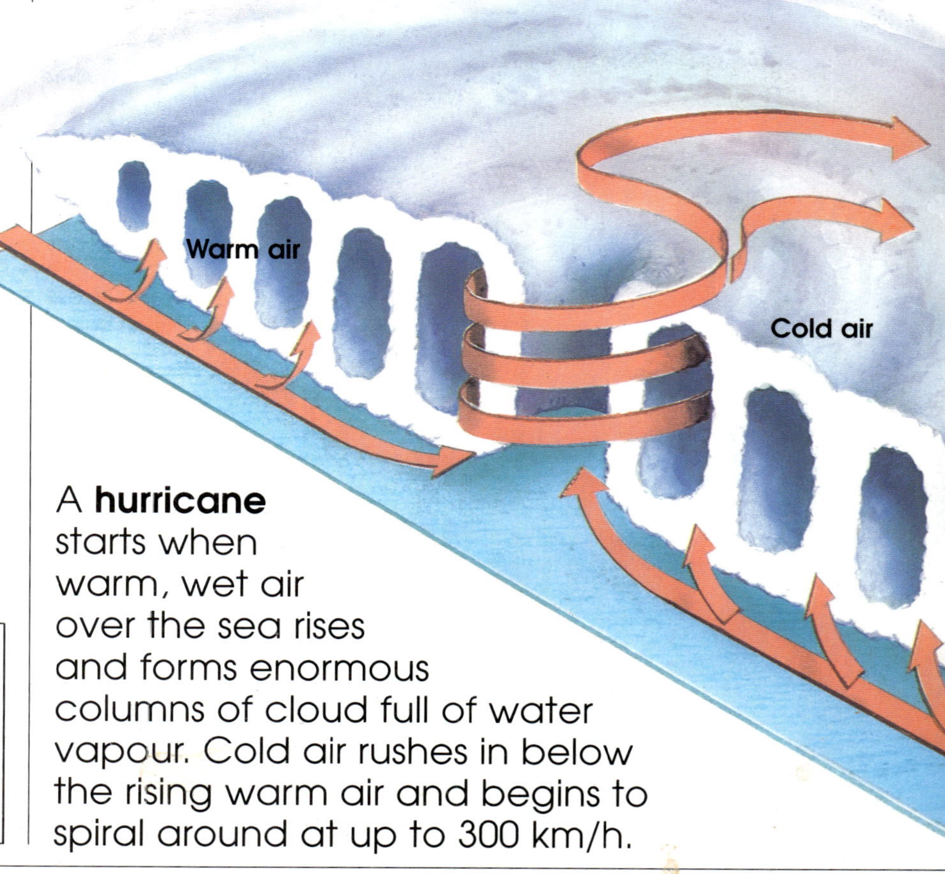

A **hurricane** starts when warm, wet air over the sea rises and forms enormous columns of cloud full of water vapour. Cold air rushes in below the rising warm air and begins to spiral around at up to 300 km/h.

Every hurricane is given a **name** to identify it. The names are chosen in alphabetical order, alternating between male and female names for each new storm. **Hurricane Gilbert** was the most powerful hurricane this century.

In 1991, a cyclone disaster killed almost 139,000 people in **Bangladesh**. Winds of 230 km/h caused floods over 1,300 sq km. Ten million people were made homeless, and four million risked death from starvation.

A **tornado** is a funnel-shaped cloud which descends from storm clouds to the ground, sucking up dust and debris as it moves. Tornadoes can tear trees out of the ground and make buildings explode.

About 200 tornadoes a year are recorded across the US. They are a major hazard in the Mississippi Valley, which is sometimes known as **Tornado Alley**.

Tornado Alley

Mexico

Caribbean

In May 1986, in **China**, it was reported that 13 schoolchildren had been sucked up into a tornado and carried 19 km before being dropped gently to the ground again.

Floods

A flood is an overflow of water. This can result from heavy rainfall, high tides, overflowing rivers or a sudden melting of snow.

Throughout history floods have caused more death and destruction than any other natural disaster on this planet.

The Bible story of **Noah** tells of a great flood that destroyed every living thing, except the family and animals on the ark.

In 1993, there was severe flooding in the **Mid-west US**. The Mississippi and Missouri rivers burst their banks along a stretch of 800 km, killing over 40 people and submerging 40,000 sq km of land. The president announced it to be a major disaster area.

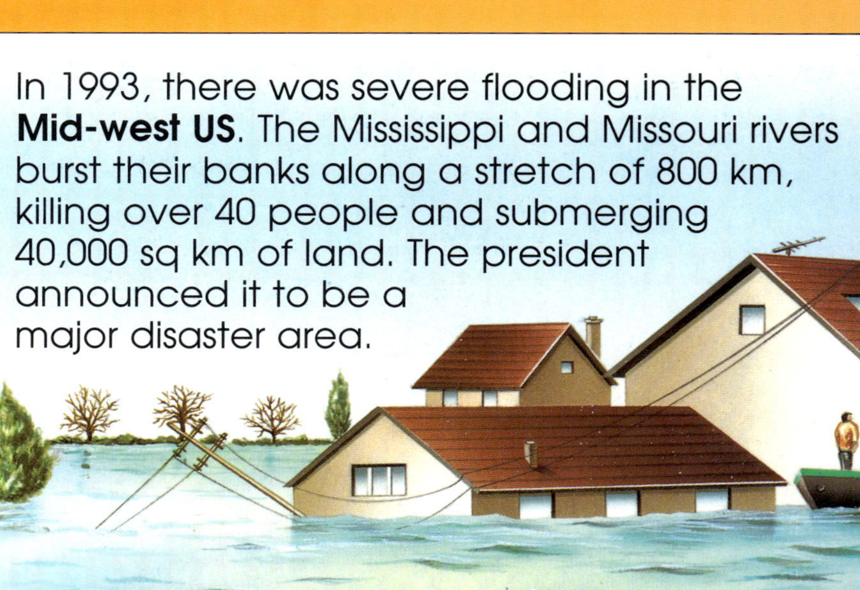

In **1994-5**, there were more floods across the world than there have been for many years.

Northern Italy had the most ferocious rainstorms of the century. Over 100 people died.

In **Germany**, the River Rhine became three times deeper than normal and flooded the city of Cologne.

In **China**, freak rainstorms made thousands of people homeless.

In **Northern Spain** houses were flooded, and a bridge collapsed.

Greece suffered from heavy flooding.

In **Egypt**, floods killed hundreds and caused damage of £1.7 billion.

In **Africa**, flash floods hit drought areas. The cocoa crops of West and Central Africa were destroyed.

Huge seas washed away roads in Victoria, **Australia**.

In **India**, 192 people died, and 40,000 people were made homeless after rainfall caused by a cyclone.

The Huang River is known as 'China's Sorrow' because it has caused the world's worst floods. In 1887, in the city of **Zhengzhou**, over one million people died, either by drowning or from the terrible disease and starvation which followed.

Low-lying land near the sea is at risk from floods at high tide. The Dutch have built many **dykes** to protect their land below sea level.

In January 1995, 250,000 people fled their homes in the Netherlands as the worst floods in nearly sixty years swept across large areas of Europe. The country's dykes were threatened and some were close to collapse.

Bangladesh, in Asia, suffers from terrible floods when cyclones sweep in from the Bay of Bengal, causing high tides and heavy rain. Nearly all of Bangladesh is on the floodplain of the Ganges and Brahmaputra rivers.

The **Thames Barrier** was built across the River Thames in London, UK, to prevent the surges of the tide from flooding the city.

Avalanches and landslides

Torrential rainfall and earthquakes often trigger off landslides, which can cause terrible destruction.

Avalanches often happen after prolonged snowfalls. They can be caused by the slightest noise.

In the Alps, during **World War I**, 10,000 soldiers lost their lives in one day in a series of snow slides.

An **avalanche** is a mass of loosened snow and earth which slips down a mountainside, growing in size as it travels.

In January, 1718, the Swiss village of **Leukerbad** was engulfed by a huge avalanche. Over 50 houses disappeared, and 52 villagers were buried under a blanket of snow.

Avalanches are a danger in any mountainous area with bare slopes and heavy snow. Where slopes have been cleared of trees for skiing or farming, walls and snow fences are built to break up any avalanche that might develop.

In **winter sports areas**, snow patrols keep a special watch and give warnings of possible avalanches to ski resorts. All roads and ski fields are closed at any sign of danger.

In 1970, on **Mount Huascaran**, Peru, an earthquake caused a gigantic **rock** and **mudslide**. It covered 14 km in less than four minutes and wiped out towns and villages in its path. A dam burst, rivers flooded and 186,000 buildings were destroyed. It was estimated that 20,000 people died and 200,000 were made homeless.

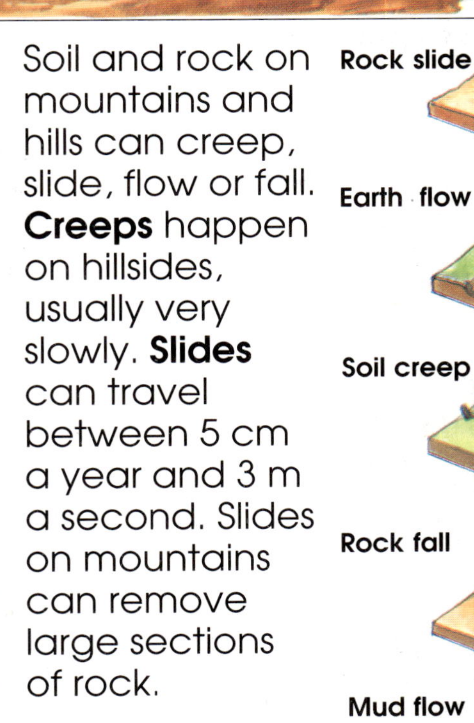

Soil and rock on mountains and hills can creep, slide, flow or fall. **Creeps** happen on hillsides, usually very slowly. **Slides** can travel between 5 cm a year and 3 m a second. Slides on mountains can remove large sections of rock.

Drought

A drought is a shortage of rain. In parts of the world where there are long periods of dry weather, droughts are common.

This means that trees and crops die, and so there is a shortage of food.

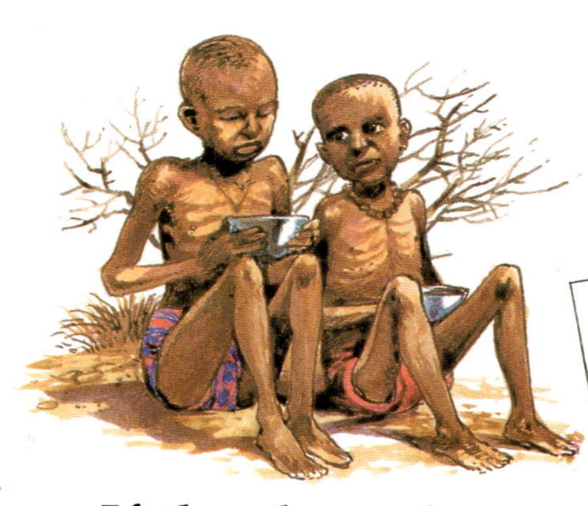

If the drought continues for a long time there is a famine in the land and many people die of starvation.

In 1770, millions of Indians died of hunger when **drought** ruined their harvests. In 1877, nearly ten million Chinese lives were lost in a famine. In the twentieth century, thousands of Africans have died of starvation when crops were ruined and cattle starved to death.

The plains of Oklahoma and Texas, in the US, were once covered in lush grass. Then the farmers ploughed them up to plant wheat. In 1930, a drought killed all the crops, and strong winds blew away the top soil. Nothing could be grown there, and the area was called **The Dust Bowl**. Later the land was reclaimed and today is no longer a desert.

During droughts up to 100 sq km of land may become desert every day.

When plants die the soil is exposed to the wind, and may easily be blown away. Green grasslands can soon turn into deserts. This is called **desertification**. It is worst in areas where people overgraze land with their large herds of cattle, or cut down trees and shrubs.

In Africa, the dry grassland of **the Sahel** suffers frequently from drought. The cattle die and the people starve.

To bring water to land devastated by drought people dig **irrigation channels**. These bring water to the land so that crops can grow.

Forest fires

When droughts cause plants to dry up, they can catch fire easily.

Lightning from a storm or a lighted cigarette can start a fire that destroys thousands of square kilometres of forest.

In the autumn of 1993, a series of bush fires raged across **California**, on the west coast of the US. Many rich and famous Hollywood stars watched as their homes went up in flames.

In January 1994, high temperatures and hot winds fanned the worst **bush fires** ever known in **Australia**. Over 130 fires raged around Sydney and the coast of New South Wales, destroying hundreds of homes. The heat was so intense it caused windows to melt and houses to explode. Over 7,500 firefighters battled with the blaze which stretched for 960 km and burned over 400,000 hectares of land. Miraculously, only four people died.

In some large forests there are tall **look-out towers** where foresters can spot the first signs of fire. Observers in helicopters fly over the fire and note its size. Then they quickly transport firefighters and equipment to the scene of the fire to fight the blaze.

During the 1994 bush fires in Australia, most of the wildlife which lived in the surrounding national parks was wiped out, including entire colonies of **koalas**. The animals that did manage to flee had no food or shelter.

Some scientists feel that fire is nature's way of renewing the land. In 1988, fires raged through **Yellowstone Park**, in the US. Many people wanted the fires put out, but as there was no property in danger they were allowed to burn. After the fires were over, the vegetation grew again very quickly.

The main tree in Yellowstone Park is the **Lodgepole pine**. The cones on this tree depend on fire because they need a minimum temperature of 45°C to open and so release their seeds.

Ice ages are periods when great sheets of ice extend far beyond the land and sea they cover today.

The Earth has experienced many ice ages, some lasting for over 100 million years.

During an ice age, sheets of ice cover large parts of the world and the level of the sea is much lower than it is now.

Ice sheets and **glaciers** erode or wear away the land they move over. The ice drags pieces of rock from the land beneath it. These rocks can be carried for kilometres before they are dropped.

This glacier is moving slowly down the valley.

The ice sheets that covered much of North America and Europe during the last ice age were up to 3,000 m thick. The ice covering the continent of **Antarctica** today is even thicker.

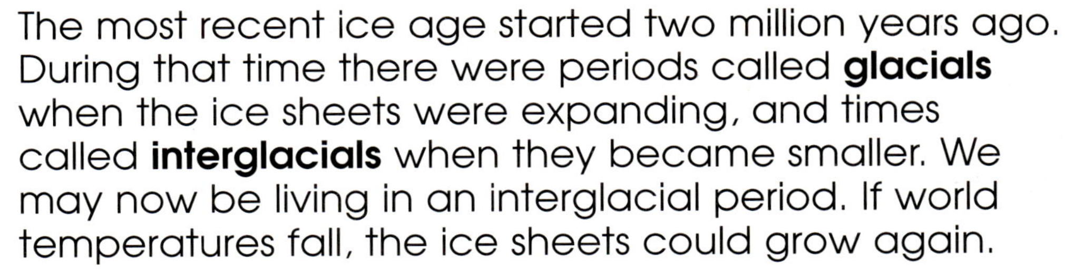

The most recent ice age started two million years ago. During that time there were periods called **glacials** when the ice sheets were expanding, and times called **interglacials** when they became smaller. We may now be living in an interglacial period. If world temperatures fall, the ice sheets could grow again.

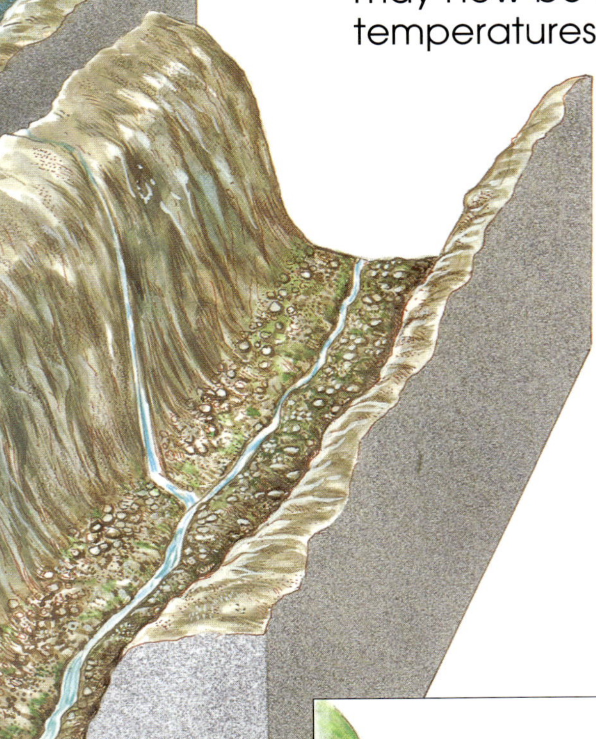

When the glacier melts it leaves a valley in the land.

Woolly mammoths lived on Earth during the recent ice age, and became extinct about 10,000 years ago.

The **fjords**, or deep sea inlets along the coast of Scandinavia were made by glaciers during the last ice age.

Approximately 18,000 years ago, towards the end of the **last ice age**, the world's climate changed dramatically. The Earth became drier, deserts grew larger and tropical rainforests shrank. Parts of South America which now have rainforests were covered in moving sand dunes.

Sea dangers

The sea has always held many dangers for sailors and other voyagers. High winds during storms create huge waves in mid-ocean. These can drive ships off their course, or wreck them on rocks and seashores.

In April 1912, the ***Titanic***, the most luxurious ocean liner of its time, set sail from Southampton, England on her maiden voyage to New York City, USA. One dark night the ship collided with an enormous **iceberg**, which ripped a hole in her side 90 m long. About 1,500 people were left stranded on the liner which quickly sank beneath the waves. It was the worst shipping disaster of all time.

Waterspouts, tidal waves, icebergs and pack ice are hazards which can cause great loss of life.

Icebergs from **Antarctica** are low, flat-topped and cover a large area.

Icebergs in the **north Atlantic** are tall, jagged, and mostly hidden beneath the waves.

A **waterspout** is a column of rising water which forms when a tornado descends over the sea. Waterspouts are often seen off the coast of the Gulf of Mexico and over the Atlantic Ocean, near Florida, USA. They suck up huge amounts of sea water into a great black cloud. Boats floating on the sea can be sucked up too.

Pack ice in the Arctic Ocean and around Antarctica can trap or crush ships. Some of the vessels used by the polar explorers were lost in this way. Nowadays, specially built **ice-breakers** can force their way through.

50m

34m

The **biggest wave** ever recorded in the open sea was seen from a ship during a storm in 1933. It was estimated to be 34 m high.

The huge volcanic eruption of **Krakatoa**, in August 1883, caused enormous waves, called **tsunamis**, to form in the sea. These swept towards the shores of Java and Sumatra, sucking up more water as they travelled. The gigantic waves, more than 50 m high, crashed down on the coast, destroying 300 villages and drowning 36,000 people.

Plagues

A plague is a very contagious disease which spreads quickly, killing many people.

Many diseases can spread rapidly if people do not take special care to stop this happening. Any illness that causes many members of a community to be ill at the same time is called an epidemic.

Nowadays, travellers and holidaymakers have **injections** to protect them from catching diseases when they visit foreign countries.

Between 1334 and 1351, a terrible epidemic, **the Black Death**, swept across Asia and Europe, killing millions of people. The disease was a form of **bubonic plague** and was spread by black rats which boarded trading ships. It was the fleas that lived on the rats which carried the plague, but unfortunately no-one realised this at the time.

Another insect which carries disease is the mosquito. **Malaria** is passed on by the bite of a mosquito which lives in tropical and sub-tropical areas.

Although there are medicines which can keep malaria at bay, no one has found a cure for it. Millions still die from the disease each year.

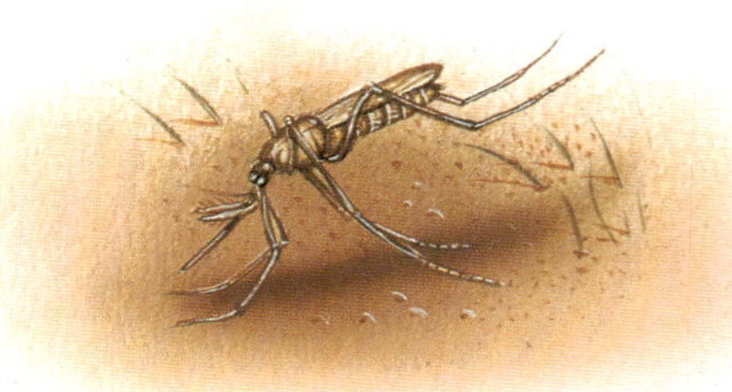

Leprosy is a disease which can be infectious. It occurs mainly in tropical and subtropical regions. It is a terrible disease which causes disfigurement.

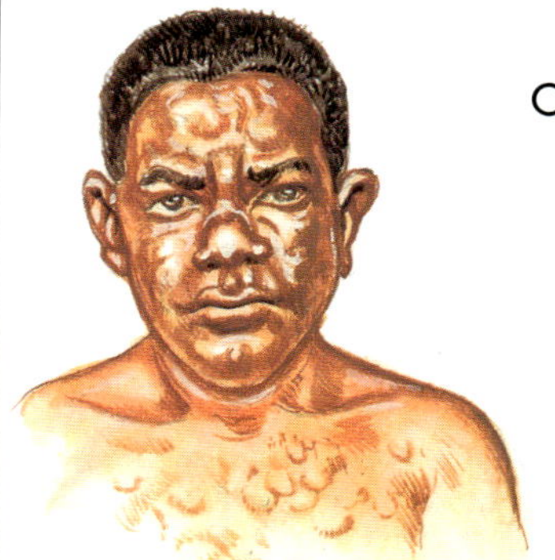

The disease can now be treated, but in the past, **lepers** were sent away from the community to live together in **leper colonies**.

In 1994, **plague** broke out in **India**. This, too, was spread by fleas, carried by rats. Nowadays, the disease can be treated with medicine called **antibiotics** if it is detected early enough.

After World War I ended in 1918, another great disaster swept across the world. A very severe kind of **influenza** killed 21 million people in four months. This was more than had been killed in the war.

Epidemics of **cholera** are common in Asia. Between 1898 and 1907, 370,000 people in India died of this disease,which is often caused by drinking dirty water.

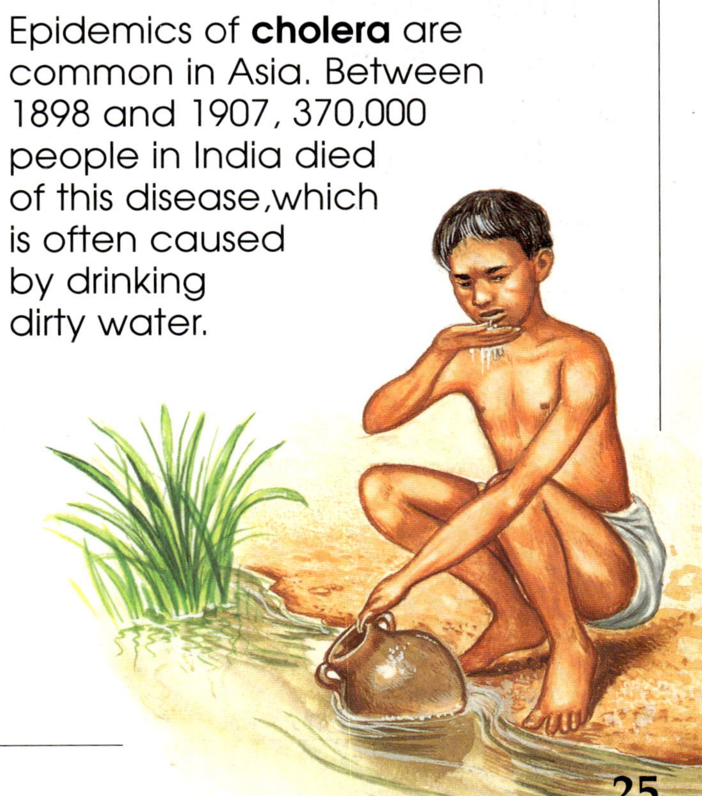

Plant and animal pests

Throughout history natural disasters have been caused by insect or animal pests, which destroy the crops on which humans live.

Some of these disasters are caused by people changing the creatures' habitats, by farming the land or by introducing new animals into areas where they were previously unknown.

One of the worst pests in Africa is the **quelea bird**. These small brown birds live together in large flocks and can destroy crops. Sometimes two million pairs can be found in an area of about 50 hectares.

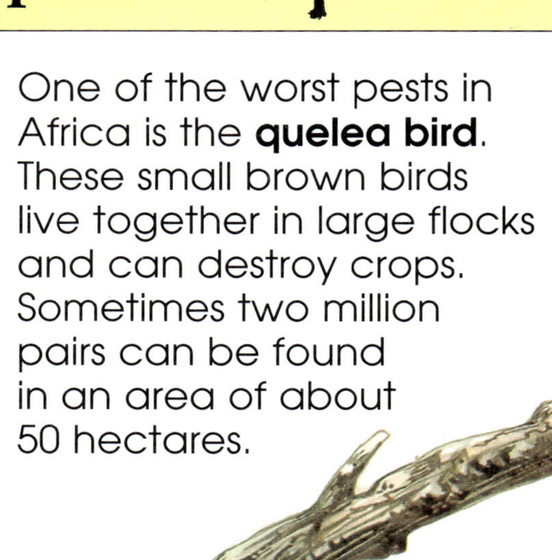

In 1889, a swarm of locusts seen flying over the **Red Sea** was roughly 5,000 sq km in size.

Locusts are giant grasshoppers which can fly long distances and travel in vast swarms. When they land, they devour the crops for miles around, causing great destruction and often widespread famine.

In the 1840s, there was a terrible disease, or **blight**, on the potato crops in Ireland. As many people lived only on these vegetables, there was a terrible shortage of food, known as the **Potato Famine**.

Dutch Elm disease has killed thousands of elm trees throughout the world. It is spread by the **European elm bark beetle**. Young trees can die within two months.

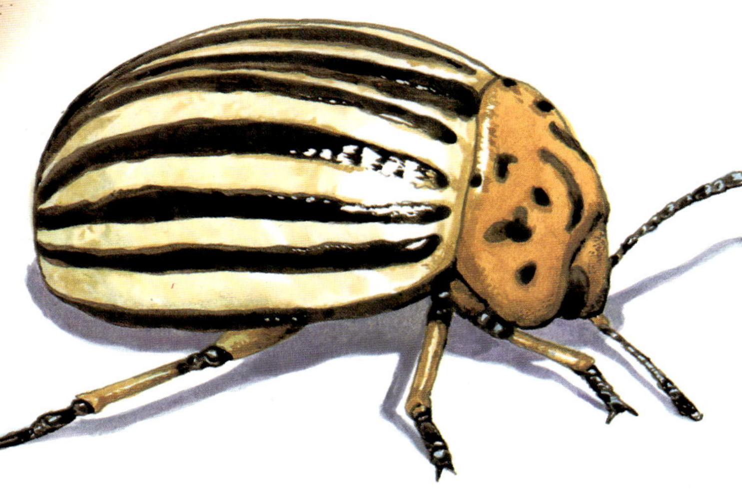

The Colorado beetle, or potato bug, is an insect pest that feeds on the leaves of potato plants in western North America. Originally, the insect fed on a wild plant which grows in the Rocky Mountains. But since potato plants were introduced into the US, it has preferred to eat those instead.

In the nineteenth century, English settlers took **rabbits** to Australia with them. Some of these eventually escaped to the outback, where they started a colony of wild rabbits, which was to become one of Australia's greatest pests. They ate farmers' crops, turned grassland into desert and their warrens caused the ground to collapse.

In the 1930s, the **cane toad** was introduced into Queensland, Australia, in order to control beetles. Now the toads are a pest!

World pollution

Over the past hundred years, industry and modern technology have changed the world. Because of these changes, many new forms of pollution now affect our planet.

Many nations have begun to act to combat pollution. But we still need stricter laws to stop any further damage.

Many factories and power plants produce **toxic waste**. This is released into the environment and poisons rivers and lakes. The creatures that live in and around these waterways die or grow deformed.

The burning of forests increases the carbon dioxide in the air, and means that there are fewer trees to absorb this gas.

Oil tankers spill vast amounts of crude oil into the sea, poisoning everything that lives there. These are called **oil slicks**.

As we pollute the atmosphere by burning fossil fuels, we also poison our rain, sleet and snow. **Acid rain** has killed forests and freshwater fish in many parts of the world. It also eats away at stone buildings and corrodes anything made of steel.

If we do not stop pollution, scientists think the average world **temperature** will rise dramatically over the next 50 years. This could cause the polar **ice-caps** to melt, flooding large areas of the world. Other areas would have terrible droughts.

Low-lying parts of London could be flooded if the average world temperature rose.

We burn the **fossil fuels** in factories, cars and power plants. These cause pollution and increase the amount of **carbon dioxide** in the air. This gas keeps heat in the **atmosphere** around the Earth. We call this **global warming**. The Sun's rays are trapped within the atmosphere just as they are in a greenhouse. So, the warming of the planet is called the **greenhouse effect**.

Some aerosols and refrigerators give off chemicals called CFCs into the atmosphere. These are damaging the **ozone layer**, which protects us from the Sun's dangerous **ultra-violet** rays. The use of CFCs has now been banned.

Danger from space

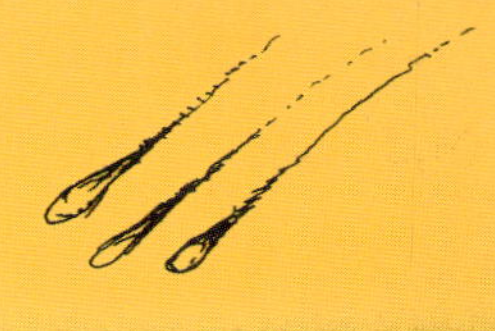

Some scientists believe that, 65 million years ago, a meteorite fell to Earth from space.

They think that the effects of the crash damaged our planet so badly that the dinosaurs became extinct.

If a similar collision happened today, it could threaten the human race.

Every year the Earth attracts more than a million tonnes of new material from space. These are called **meteors**. Most meteors disintegrate before they reach the ground, but sometimes the core survives and is called a **meteorite**.

If, as some scientists think, a large meteorite did hit the Earth millions of years ago, it would have thrown up a huge cloud of dust. This would have lowered the temperature and eventually killed most of the plant and animal life.

   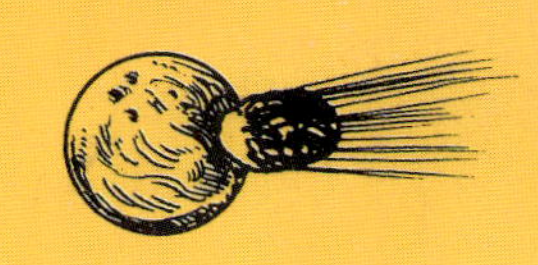

In **Arizona**, USA, there is a gigantic crater in the ground, caused by a meteor measuring about 30 m across. It must have been travelling at a speed of about 50,000 km/h because the meteor struck the ground with such force it made a crater nearly 200 m deep and 1.2 km wide.

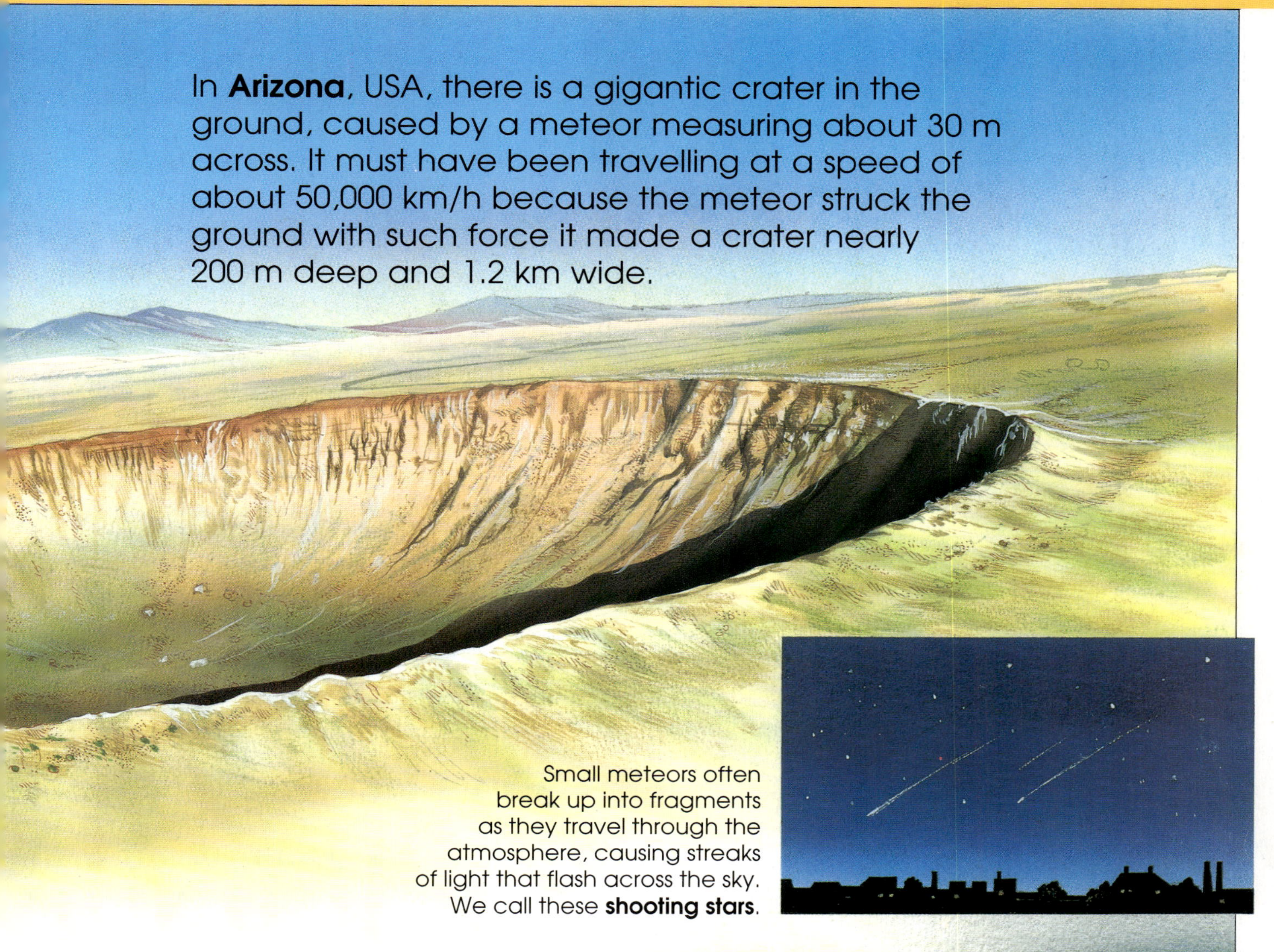

Small meteors often break up into fragments as they travel through the atmosphere, causing streaks of light that flash across the sky. We call these **shooting stars**.

In July 1994, 21 giant particles of rock and ice from the comet **Shoemaker-Levy 9**, collided with the planet **Jupiter**. One of the fragments created a giant fire-ball and Earth-sized hole in the planet's atmosphere. The US government has given scientists fifty million dollars to create an early warning system to predict such a thing happening to the Earth.

Index

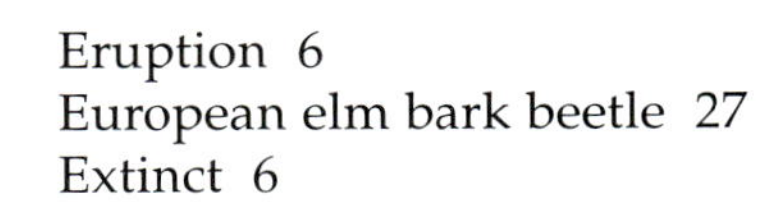

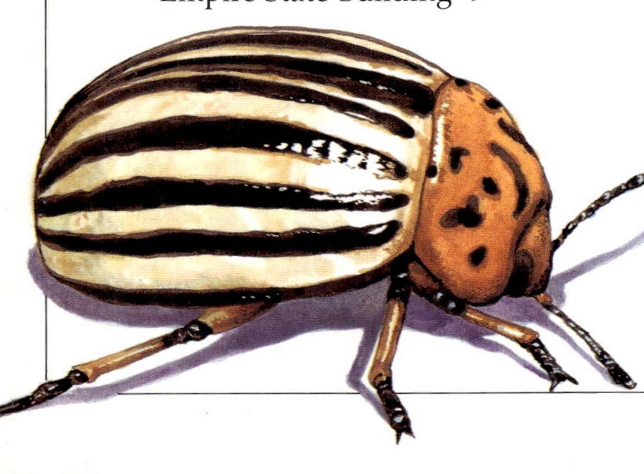